After Ninety

Cover: Imogen's Hands
Endpapers: Imogen Photographing
Drawings by Ruth Asawa

My Father at Ninety

After Ninety

IMOGEN CUNNINGHAM

Introduction by Margaretta Mitchell

UNIVERSITY OF WASHINGTON PRESS
Seattle and London

Library of Congress Cataloging in Publication Data

Cunningham, Imogen, 1883-1976.
    After ninety.

    Bibliography: p.
1. Photography, Artistic.   2. Photography—Portraits.
I. Mitchell, Margaretta.   II. Title.
TR654.C86   779'.2   77-73306
ISBN 0-295-95559-7
ISBN 0-295-95673-9 (pbk.)

Publisher's Foreword

After Ninety is the third book by Imogen Cunningham we have had the privilege of publishing. Though she had originally planned to publish a third book from earlier photographs, at the age of ninety-two Imogen decided that it was time to create a new body of work. This book is the result of that decision, and with only a few exceptions contains photographs made by Imogen since her last publication. Until her death in June 1976 at ninety-three she was an active and lively participant in the book's development, as she had been with the other two, *Imogen Cunningham: Photographs* and *Imogen! Imogen Cunningham Photographs 1910-1973*. Although the idea for the book had apparently been in her mind for some time before, the title, "After Ninety," emerged in the course of a conversation with her publisher in October 1975, and that was how the work in progress was always referred to thereafter.

As an author Imogen was exacting but not obstructive, interested in every phase of the physical design of the book, the evolution of the textual content, and, of course, the quality of reproduction of the photographs. Her comments, conveyed by letter or telephone, were typically tart, incisive, and—whether quotable or unquotable—delightful. A true professional herself, she respected and had confidence in the professionalism of others in a field in which she was something of a neophyte.

Imogen's death cut short her participation in this last book, and it could not have been completed without the contributions of devoted friends and collaborators. Adrian Wilson, acting as far more than book designer and production supervisor, played the leading role in the final selection and arrangement of the photographs and in devising the captions, which are based for the most part on Imogen's own comments as taped by Adrian and Joyce Wilson. Margaretta Mitchell has set forth her own indebtedness to those whose information and recollection are woven into her eloquent evocation of Imogen in her many roles, both in a literal sense and as a symbolic, almost mythical, figure of the aged in our society. And the indispensable cooperation of The Imogen Cunningham Trust must also be noted.

It was our good fortune as Imogen's publishers to be with her to celebrate publication of her two earlier books, the first at a gala champagne opening in the de Young Museum, followed by a small dinner for family members, friends, and a few close associates at one of San Francisco's Chinese restaurants; the second at a never-to-be-forgotten picnic in the walled garden behind the Press building in Seattle. This Foreword must stand, all too inadequately, in place of a third celebration.

Acknowledgments

In the research for this text, I could reach only a fraction of the many persons Imogen counted as friends. Still there were many with whom I spoke, some for hours, others for minutes. Each person gave me something unique, building a picture of Imogen that went beyond that of my own brief acquaintance with her. I knew Imogen, bought prints from her, passed several long afternoons in conversations with her, observed her at parties, but that is not enough, not for a life of ninety-three years. Thus, I extend my real thanks to these friends and associates who helped me so freely to bring Imogen's life into focus: Ansel Adams, Ruth Asawa, Judy Dater, Margo Davis, Dorothea Dunham, Tom Eckstrom, Peg Frankel, Ann Hershey, Chris Johnson, Margery Mann, Danee McFarr, Arthur and Lillie Mayer, Anita Mozley, Gryffyd Partridge, Padraic Partridge, Roi Partridge, Rondal Partridge, Arthur Shartsis, Paul S. Taylor, Michelle Vignes, Alma Lavenson Wahrhaftig, Irwin Welcher, Adrian and Joyce Wilson.

I am also indebted to several persons for discussion on the subject of aging: Christopher Kiefer, associate professor of anthropology in the Human Development Program at the University of California Medical School, San Francisco; Gay Gaer Luce, psychologist, author, and founder and codirector of SAGE (Senior Actualization and Growth Explorations); Katharine Whiteside Taylor, clinical psychologist, educator, and author (and in her eightieth year herself.)

In the practical preparation of the manuscript I am grateful for all the support and assistance I received. I want to mention especially my husband and unofficial editor, Frederick C. Mitchell, and those who typed the manuscripts, Millea Kenin and Annette Wikner.

I want to thank my friends at the University of Washington Press, as well as the trustees of The Imogen Cunningham Trust, whose work on *After Ninety* is felt in every aspect of preparation. For all of us this has been an opportunity to celebrate Imogen in the best way possible, by working.

Finally, most important of all, we all want to express gratitude to those who posed for Imogen, the fine folk whose presence here makes a worthy portrait of old age.

Margaretta Mitchell

Berkeley, California
April 1977

Imogen and Her City. Photograph by Tom Eckstrom

Introduction

"Let us recognize ourselves in this old man or in that old woman. It must be done if we are to take upon ourselves the entirety of our human state."

Simone de Beauvoir, *The Coming of Age*

In any society the destiny of the aged is decided by the community and reflects its deepest human values, which on the individual level speak to the value each of its members places on his or her own life. The fate of those who are now old is there waiting for the next generation. In civilizations concerned with maintaining their traditions, the old retain power; their memories, which preserve the traditions, give them a special place in the society. They are admired for the great number of years they have lived, respected for their wisdom, and in some cases feared for their presumed supernatural powers. In such a society the aged may become sacred, priests and priestesses with powers similar to those possessed by ghosts, the spirits they soon will become.

Western civilization, spending vast amounts on medical research to keep people alive, has made tremendous advances in extending the physical life of its people. But old age in our society is too often viewed with horror, especially by Americans, as a reminder of death in a culture where death is a terribly final act. There are, to be sure, numerous examples of individuals who manage to lead creative and productive lives well after the arbitrary retirement age of sixty-five. Nevertheless, as a society we have failed to create a healthy and useful population of old people, but are too often left instead with a sad army of bored and useless men and women, living tidy half-lives characterized by separation from active society and sterile, hospital-like care. These are the helpless victims of the stereotyped view that sees them as physically and mentally feeble, their knowledge out of date, their interests irrelevant to what is happening now, their ability to contribute to our fast-paced consumer society a thing of the past. "When you come here nobody knows where you are," said one woman who was photographed by Imogen Cunningham in a "convalescent home."

No words can describe old age as well as the photographs reproduced in *After Ninety*, which is a direct result of Imogen's own confrontation with life after ninety. This is surely one of the most unusual projects ever undertaken by a photographer, not only because few artists live or work to such a fine old age, but also because in our culture it is the rare artist of any age whose work confronts this stage of life without fear, without condescension, but with self-identification and compassion. Imogen herself, as she turned ninety, became a living symbol of youth in old age, still making new portraits, printing almost every morning, and keeping up with the latest work of other photographers near and far. Her work was not just her picture-making; it was people as well. This book is witness to the fact that she never gave up that work.

We saw her striding around San Francisco, easily recognized by the beaded cap atop a fringe of white bangs and the black cape winging behind her intent little figure. The message she conveyed was hopeful and reassuring: that it was possible to grow old, working; to maintain interest in life; to be energetic; to be wholly oneself—in short, to love one's destiny.

Imogen considered herself a worker; when asked about her philosophy of life, she simply replied: "The goal of life is to get a lot of work done each day," and she did. According to her last assistant, "She worked seven days a week, ten hours a day. Work was her philosophy, but she didn't talk about it. She talked with and about people. Her work made her single-minded, but it also gave her energy to live in the present. All her life she dealt with things as they came, nothing pompous, nothing indirect. As an old person she was still young. She didn't think she had answers; that was 'bunk,' she'd say. To her, she was just doing what she wanted to do. Very simple. Just plenty of work; living out the answers in her work."

She had recognized the significance of work for women as early as 1913, when she wrote an article on "Photography as a Profession for Women"*: "Fortunately, we have long passed the stage when there is any disgrace attached to work: if a woman wishes to work, she is not regarded as eccentric; if she is obliged to, it is not a misfortune."

Her work kept her young. Because of it she never had much to do with others of her own age. "After all," she said, "haven't you noticed what my contemporaries are doing? Talking about their arthritis." Meanwhile, she had been developing a different image of herself, one she saw mirrored in a community of young photographers, students, and friends who shared her interests. Much visited, she drew people to her, to her modest house in San Francisco—a three-room shack, she called it—set high above the street behind a dense green patch of garden identified by a giant palm tree in the center. Most of her work of the past twenty-nine years had taken place there, and those who knew her well could not imagine her anywhere else. She lived alone, spending her time photographing, working on her endless correspondence (much of it fan mail), finishing pictures, visiting, lecturing, reading, gardening, and cooking. She arose early and lived simply.

The Imogen Cunningham reflected in the eyes and remembrances of her ever widening circle of friends was not an old person. An old person—in the view of so many in our society, including Imogen herself—was alone, lonely, dependent, passive, and dull. Since in no way did she want to be that kind of person, she could not think of herself as old—even if she looked it.

Seen among her friends and followers, she might be described as presiding over a latter-day salon, in her own magnetic manner, with a peppery, irreverent wit; a constant curiosity about people; and a look that was straight, that measured and weighed you inside and out. Whether in her living room or at an opening of an exhibition of photographs, she was always holding forth at the center of a ring of admirers. If you had nerve enough to speak up, upon seeing her, you might be the recipient of that sharp tongue, almost always sassy, or clever, or devilishly blunt. Indeed, she might turn her sharp twin lenses on you, tease you into a portrait sitting, or invite you in from the porch of her cottage for lunch.

*Complete citations for this and other sources quoted in the Introduction will be found in the Bibliography, p. 109.

Age was not relevant. When a friend asked her to come to visit her disabled mother, Imogen's response was: "I wish I could, but you and I would have such fun, and your poor mother would be so neglected." (Imogen was at that time ninety-one, her friend fifty-six, and the mother eighty-six.) If she was like "a teenager for the first eighty-nine years of her life," as it seemed to young friends running to keep up with her, then the shock of future physical limitations and the narrowing of possibilities must have been greater for her than for the average ninety-year-old, long accustomed to the ailments of aging. Returning from her ninety-second birthday picnic in the country, she turned to her friends Ruth Asawa and Albert Lanier and asked, "Don't you think I've aged?" At such advanced years the question was almost amusing, and Imogen was impish enough to know it.

Imogen set out to photograph only people over the age of ninety, but she found that too many elderly people were interesting and just had to be included even if they were somewhat younger. As with all her work, the idea developed naturally out of her own interest, her eye found the subject, and the project enlarged with her perception of it. When she went to see homes for the aged, she did not like what she saw, and she became progressively aware of the true situation confronting many elderly persons in our culture. So often they had become dependent, as a result of circumstances over which they had lost control, but Imogen sought out individuals whose independent spirits had managed to transcend their problems.

These photographs are a kind of visual research, straightforward studies of the way people are at the end of life, revealed in a face, an expression, a gesture, a posture. If Imogen recognized that there was a risk in the discoveries revealed to her, she might have said, after ninety, who cares? . . . the subject is beyond art. Aesthetically speaking, old age lacks the mystery of death itself; it is rather a well-worn slope declining along the ragged edge of time when no standards of beauty need apply any longer and no elegance of design can temper the faded physical expression of the person. Truth wins out in the end. All through her life, Imogen the photographer was motivated not by external beauty but by the vulnerable human core of personality, the human spirit. If she sought truth, it was about herself as well as her subject.

Never a worshiper of beauty for its own sake, Imogen had expressed herself on the subject as early as her 1913 article, showing how much ahead of her time she was as an artist and as a woman. The rest of her life was a living out of these attitudes, as true for the artist today as they were then. She wrote of finding her aesthetic satisfaction in a search for "beauty in the commonest things." She added that "accomplishments in any art are all a matter of gradual growth, not only in the individual but in the age . . . in photography thought and judgment are paramount. The drawing is done by the lens . . . it takes more than a mere automaton to squeeze the bulb and get a defined, determined and pleasing result. The technique must be mastered."

She tells where she would look for subjects: "If one decides upon the medium of photography, why attempt to soar in the realm of the imagination? . . . There are plenty of the subtleties of life right on the earth, which need delicate interpretation. . . . If photography needs any new recruits, it needs only people of good taste who know the fitness of things and have a sense of the limitations of the medium. And with this good taste should be combined the hand of the skilled mechanic, the eye of an artist and the brains of a scientist. By these requirements I do not mean that a person who does not have them cannot succeed; but I do mean that the more of them he has, the greater the possibility of his success. Some may have a devotion to science, the skill of hand, and the seeing eye, without knowing it. It may be the gift of the gods, but most of it comes from a determination to use what one has and make that little grow in as many broadening directions as possible."

It was her firm belief even then that a woman should find her "real work," not just work to imitate men in society. "I am willing to work for bread or for the love of work—but not to oblige illogical theorists!" she concluded. Within this series of statements about her chosen profession are the basic tenets of her life work, written when she was thirty years old.

As a young woman artist, Imogen spoke of her photography simply as work, and she shared that work with others. She let it speak for itself. Gregarious by nature, she must nevertheless have accustomed herself to the burden of loneliness commonly felt by artists, who live near the source of creative energy, the unconscious, and can so easily become neurotically detached from everyday life. Imogen always had her feet on the ground and her hands in the dirt. She had a practical nature much like that of her father, her lifelong inspiration, who once told her that when he was no longer useful he would turn his head to the wall. "He died at ninety-eight without any organic disease," Imogen said, comfortable with this matter-of-fact statement. Her profile portrait of her father, Isaac Burns Cunningham, is reminiscent of a bearded Biblical or modern prophet (Moses or Walt Whitman, or perhaps Tolstoy, whom Imogen herself mentioned as resembling him), and is one of the few idealized portraits she ever made.

By the time Imogen Cunningham was through high school she had expressed her wish to become a photographer to her father, with whom she had, she said, complete rapport. "He was a reader, and so we could talk about things. He also liked me very much." Both father and daughter were free spirits, and he respected her determination in the choice of photography as a profession even though he thought it a "dirty" business; he would have preferred that she become a teacher. By 1901 she had sent for a 4 x 5 camera and a book of instructions from the International Correspondence School in Scranton, Pennsylvania, and was working in a cold-water darkroom which her father had built for her in the woodshed, made light-tight by lining the walls with black tarpaper.

Her fascination with photography as an art form took hold when she saw reproductions of the photographs of Gertrude Käsebier. She always made special mention of Mrs. Käsebier's "Blessed Art Thou among Women," an allegorical photograph of a mother and daughter in a doorway, referring to the Biblical scene of the Visitation. When later, in 1910, she met Gertrude Käsebier in New York, it must have satisfied Imogen's desire to see at close hand her inspiration, a practicing woman photographer who was, incidentally, both a mother and a portrait photographer, having taken up the medium in midlife while studying painting in Europe. The example of the older woman's determined energy may well have bolstered Imogen, if indeed she needed any reinforcement for her own determination to become a photographer. "I had strictly one idea, that of photography, after I started work with my camera."

Imogen's family came from an enduring line of sturdy Scots who emigrated to Ireland in 1608 and from there to Virginia. Gradually the clan had migrated west, to Missouri. Her father married and spent some years in Texas before he went way out west to look for a better opportunity to make a go at farming, and there he remarried after his first wife died. When asked about longevity, Imogen would always refer to her good genes. (Her father died at ninety-eight, her mother at eighty-eight, one sister at ninety-five, and another at ninety-six.) Imogen always worked, and since she was from a poor working-class family of ten children—she was the fifth child, the first of the second marriage—she was raised to be frugal as well as free-thinking. From the time she went to college she paid her keep as a matter of course while she was living at home.

She often spoke of her father as a vegetarian, a farmer, and a kind of self-styled socialist as well as a Theosophist. He tried farming, logging, road-grading, and at one time ran a wood and coal business in Seattle to support his large family. Of her mother, she never had much to say, as they had little in common; "she was almost completely illiterate."

It seems clear that Imogen was her father's favorite, and that she identified her life goals with his. He was a man of strong convictions, high social and personal standards, great intellectual curiosity, and a striking independence of spirit. She matched her father in these qualities throughout her life, as restless in her quest for self-expression as he was in his. Imprinted at an early age with these values, Imogen graduated from the University of Washington in three and a half years with honors in chemistry, which was in those days considered a man's field of study. She had wanted to major in art, but at that time there was no art department at the university. For two years she worked in the Edward S. Curtis studio in Seattle where she learned the difficult process of platinum printing. She then accepted a five-hundred-dollar Pi Beta Phi scholarship to study photochemistry at the Technische Hochschule in Dresden, Germany. After a year's study and travel, she returned to Seattle where she set up her own portrait studio.

From the very beginning, Imogen's approach to portraiture stressed her commitment to the human, rather than the heroic, quality of the subject. Her respect for differences among people would not let impressions be reduced to stereotypes; on the other hand, she rejected anything that made a man seem larger than life. With each sitter she always tried to penetrate the mask, to reach the person. Even in 1910, when she was a student in Germany, her portrait of Professor Luter was the result of his suggestion that he concentrate on a mathematical problem while she photographed: the snap of the shutter would reflect the moment of greatest mental intensity. That interaction gave her insight into a method of breaking through the self-consciousness of the sitter—a method which she continued to use, asking questions about the sitter's life and thoughts in order to obtain an expressive portrait. She said essentially the same thing, both in writing for her alumnae journal in 1913 at the beginning of her career and in her last interview, in the spring of 1976, about the requirements of fine portrait work: "You must be able to gain an understanding at short notice and at close range of the beauties of character, intellect, and spirit, so as to be able to draw out the best qualities and make them show in the face of the sitter."

Being mischievous by nature, or "nasty" as she would have called it, Imogen might treat the heroic person ironically, in jest, as she did when photographing Ansel Adams in 1953, catching him gesturing skyward from a perch on a rock, looking as if he were delivering the word of God. In private she referred to this photograph as "The Sermon on the Mount." Her favorite later portrait of Edward Weston was the informal pose of him taken in 1945 leaning casually against an outdoor table, surrounded by his many cats, whereas her earlier portrait of Weston with the photographer Margrethe Mather seemed more caught up in the process of posing, gesture, arrangement. There a touch of theater prevailed, bringing to mind another facet of Imogen's personality, one that moves steadily like a subplot throughout her career, growing into a full drama when fame reached her as a person as well as a photographer.

Throughout Imogen's life, the actress was always waiting in the wings, ready to come on and upstage the artist. As a child she had enjoyed "dressing up" and inventing plays with a friend "who had a wonderful house with a great big attic." Work and play were always synonymous to her. A delightful insight from the time she was a young woman appears on the front page of the *Seattle Post-Intelligencer*, 1 June 1913, which displays the members of the Seattle Fine Arts Society dressed up and posed to represent famous paintings. Imogen not only photographed the others but posed herself as "The Earliest Photograph," hair drawn in a bun, holding a nosegay, attired in a low-cut, full-skirted dress in the manner of the nineteenth-century portraits by David Octavius Hill and Thomas Adamson.

It is well known that a major influence on her earliest "pictorial" photographs was the work of the Photo-Secession group. She was also inspired by an enthusiasm for Pre-Raphaelite poetry and dramatic tableaux which she shared with her coterie of artist friends, and she participated fully in the romantic concepts of such artist-writers as William Morris and Dante Gabriel Rossetti, with their yearning for a symbolic return to the Middle Ages and their belief in the goodness of Nature as a principle and as a reality.

Her early work moved energetically forward on the wave of these influences. In her Seattle studio she hung blue draperies on her walls (as did Isadora Duncan) and set statues of the *Winged Victory* and the *Venus de Milo* on either side of the double brick mantle. For Seattle, it was hardly the average commercial portrait studio. It was described in the first of the many interviews Imogen granted, this one for a column in the local paper called "Successful Seattle Business Women" written by E. Isabelle Halderman. Imogen, at the age of twenty-seven, explained that she "wanted to escape the conventionalities that surround photography. The outside gives me great scope in combining landscape and portraiture. I use it both summer and winter. The out-of-doors lends an inspiration to my indoor work."

There were echoes of that earliest studio and its personal, inviting character in Imogen's small, cluttered, but charming home on the steep block of Green Street in San Francisco, where she moved in 1947 and where she lived for the rest of her life. "Her house was a very good nest," is the way one of her photographer friends put it, "and it was original, totally Imogen. Everything—her house, her garden, her clothes, the colors and textures, the food she prepared—everything was very simple and yet very refined; everywhere there were arrangements. Even the clutter had character. Everything was of an artist, you would see that she followed where her eyes and mind led her; it made a kind of beauty which was not conventional." The recollection of Imogen popping out of the tiny kitchen of her Green Street house, offering sherry and opinions to her guests, is hardly different from that of the young Miss Cunningham in a 1914 article by Flora Huntley Maschmedt, who describes her appearing from behind a screen with a cup of tea, full of discussion of "late fiction, grand opera or her friends' babies." As a matter of fact, the author continues, "there is nothing of the aggressive business woman in the appearance of this successful artist. She might have left a pie in the oven or a baby in the nursery or have just discarded her tennis racket as she comes forward to greet you. It is this humanness which gives her personal charm."

Even in the first impression in those early days, Imogen was seen at ease with herself. Because she had developed her image from such a young and unique blend of art with theater, she had ample opportunity over the long years to carry out her vision quest, the tenacity to hold onto it, and a restless mind that never quite exhausted the possibilities. She always claimed that her best photograph would be the one she would make tomorrow. She seemed youthful to the last because, like the poet Emily Dickinson, she "dwelt in possibility."

Although she was unusually well educated for a woman of her time, Imogen always defended self-education. As late as 1976, in her last interview, she spoke against the current rise of academic photographic education: "A master's degree is a waste of time. Once you learn how to print and develop, you should be on your own. They would do better learning about literature or philosophy— a well-rounded education." Asked about herself, she gave a rather ironic reply: "I won't bother you with thoughts on myself. I'm not impulsive and I don't think I'm the greatest ever. I just want to work for my own satisfaction. If anyone I ever photographed disliked my work, I'd throw it in the wastebasket in front of them and say nothing. I will not defend anything. I'm not really interested in what people are saying now about my work. Wait a hundred years."

If Imogen accepted the demands of photography as her chosen craft, she also accepted her role as a mother. Work was the bridge between the two. She was a thirty-two-year-old professional portrait photographer when she married the etcher Roi Partridge in 1915 and began to combine career with husband and children. Within a few years she had three sons, Gryffyd and the twins Padraic and Rondal. Following a move in 1917 from Seattle to the San Francisco Bay Area, Roi went to teach art at Mills College in Oakland, California, and for the rest of their marriage they lived nearby.

The college community provided the Partridges with an active social life and new subject matter for Imogen's camera. She managed to combine the tasks of mother, housewife, and photographer in her own style, producing her best-known work of the 1920s in her own back yard. Since she never drove a car, she was often confined there with her children. They aided and abetted her work, bringing snakes to be seen, holding still occasionally to help her finish a roll of film; in fact, it could be said that because of them she turned to plants for her subject matter, since gardening was a natural extension of the domestic scene as well as an escape from it. One of her most famous images is that of the "Magnolia Blossom," which Padraic recalls as having been brought home from Mills and put into a vase where it sat for at least three days before it was photographed.

When Imogen and Roi were divorced in 1934, the boys were almost grown. Her creative horizons widened as she worked for *Vanity Fair* in both New York and Hollywood, but from the 1930s to the 1960s she was primarily a portrait photographer, working hard to make a living. Although her career spanned over half the history of photography itself (her first exhibition was in 1912 at the Brooklyn Academy of Arts and Sciences), she was not well known beyond the West Coast until the 1960s. She was mainly recognized for her participation in the f/64 Group, composed of Bay Area photographers who, during the early thirties, championed the straight approach in contrast to the then-popular pictorial style.

It was with some small shreds of bitterness that Imogen spoke later about waiting until her eighties to be discovered. "I was just as good a photographer then as I am now." She applied for a Guggenehim Fellowship at the age of eighty-one to photograph "the grand dames of England,"

Ann Hershey Filming Imogen. Photograph by Tom Eckstrom

women who were well-established in the art world. She was turned down, but finally received a fellowship at eighty-seven. By then she felt beyond such travel, so she requested the grant to print some of her old work, much of which was published in 1974 in her second book, *Imogen! Imogen Cunningham Photographs 1910-1973*. This book, following the earlier *Imogen Cunningham: Photographs* (1970) helped to bring her the wider recognition that was her due. Many artists die before they are discovered. Imogen endured long enough to live her own legend.

In addition to her photographic achievements, a long life allowed Imogen the time to live out her childhood dream of becoming an actress. Ann Hershey, whose film, *Never Give Up: Imogen Cunningham,* was made by working with Imogen over a four-year period (1970-74), felt that she had the actress's love of center stage, of drawing attention to herself through the character she played, "the little old lady whose style always defied us to understand her completely." Imogen told Ann that she always blamed herself for not trying to get attached to some company when she first saw Hollywood. "If only I had thought it was the great dream I might have got in on it. Even as an actress, you know. I could have been that."

In fact, she was. She was the subject of two other films: Fred Padula's *Two Photographers, Imogen Cunningham and Wynn Bullock,* filmed in 1966, and John Korty's *Imogen Cunningham, Photographer*, filmed in 1967. She also appeared—photographing blind sculptors—in a television documentary made by David Myers in 1952, acted in James Broughton's film *The Bed* in 1967, and at ninety-three stole the "Tonight" show from Johnny Carson on television. That same spring CBS made a half-hour documentary about her. She gave her last interview in 1976, and commenting on it all in her last letter to her publisher, dated 28 May 1976, she wrote: "I am giving up vaudeville and Hollywood. I mean it."

After she embarked on this book project, Imogen discovered that all old people are survivors, all and each courageous. She searched for the active aged, those who maintained an independent spirit. It was difficult, discouraging at times, not so much because of the individuals, but because of the way she found that old age itself has been physically and psychologically separated from American culture —a situation Imogen herself had not recognized until then because she had never acknowledged her chronological age. According to her friends, it struck her that something must be wrong with our society if we are so little interested in our individual human destiny. What are our values concerning human life anyway? For the photographer this project was becoming a social document, asking us to see our natural selves now, so as not to be ashamed of our faces as they are deeply etched upon by life.

"A fine old age," wrote André Gide, "can never be taken for granted. It represents perpetual victories, and perpetual recoveries from defeat." Each of the lives symbolized in these portraits by Imogen may be viewed as such a triumph, as is the very existence of the book itself. The fact that the photographer, beginning in her ninety-second year, worked steadily until her death on 24 June 1976, seeking her subjects, photographing them, selecting and supervising the printing of the photographs, wrapping and sending complimentary prints to sitters is astonishing. Such work is full of physical effort usually considered possible only for the young or the mature adult. Indeed, Imogen always claimed a sturdy constitution, saying that it would take a Mack truck to stop her from jumping about.

More important, she had the capacity for change we so rarely expect to find in an old person. She always seemed in process, meeting new people, experimenting with different approaches to her work. To her, photography was more a process than a product, a series of experiences rather than a group of finished pieces. Hers was not an easy attitude for an art critic to tackle because she developed several bodies of work, not a consistent arrangement conveniently understandable to art historians, whose criteria for judgment usually stem from concepts drawn from the disciplines of drawing, painting, and sculpture. Photography extends those forms to other realms and demands other criteria for judgment. A person's photographic *œuvre* can be as contradictory and confusing in its development as is the person.

Imogen lived her own contradictions and spoke her mind, which was always trying out new ideas. The longer she lived, the more evident are the contradictions in her work, and the more complex are the mind and the life energy behind that mind.

For Imogen, it was important that she photograph the old people for *After Ninety* to learn something. Never interested in making pictures merely to have them judged against the work of other photographers, she seldom talked publicly about the work of her colleagues and did not much care for philosophizing about art. She was not one for comparisons; her work was measured by experience, not by some abstract concept such as style. This final project is a humble one, completely in keeping with the direction of her lifelong creative interest in the particular, in the human core of a person, and it reflects her acceptance of her own aging. There are no more prizes and awards. There is just courage, courage to look through the lens and see herself mirrored in others, always looking with a childlike curiosity, learning from another's reality ways to be strong, active, interesting, and useful.

Usually the people she found were younger than she, if only by a few years. Arthur and Lillie Mayer, ninety-one and eighty-eight years old, respectively, whom Imogen photographed in April 1976 shortly after she herself turned ninety-three, are as lively and dynamic as was Imogen. Arthur recalled that he hardly ever met people older than he who were not frail and careful, but Imogen was "just as vivacious and active as a girl. It was such a joy to meet someone that age who was able to carry on like that. I felt some of the encouragement in her presence that other people feel from us. She was a model of what I would like to be at ninety-three." Of the portrait sitting he said: "She relaxed us with great skill. In fact, we seemed to feel like intimate friends in a very short time. She was encouraging, got us to talk, gave us self-reliance. The next thing we knew, we were talking as if she were an old friend. Usually photographers try to get you to look cheerful, happy, gay. They say, 'Smile, please for the birdie.' She made no such effort. I think the picture is the only serious picture I ever had made of me. I like it very much, but my children loathe it. They want papa laughing, smiling, you know, happy."

Downright honest, Imogen rarely attempted to idealize people, but she also did not devalue them. Her portraits have integrity in their natural humanity. Never having been considered a beauty herself, Imogen had long ago accepted her face. She not only was not ashamed of her aging physiognomy, but she loved to be photographed, to play the character she had created. She wanted that freedom from the vanity of physical beauty for those she photographed. It could be said that through her portraits she wanted others to deal with this acceptance as she had herself. As she stated in the 1961 interview, "I'm always agonized during a sitting because in photography, you can never be sure that you're getting the intangibles." This was a theme reiterated in recorded conversations throughout her life, for as she said in a more recent interview, "I've made my living photographing people for their portraits. And it's a very fragile kind of living because people do not like themselves. They say, 'You photographed the wrong side of my face.'"

Imogen Photographing Arthur and Lillie Mayer
Photograph by Margo Davis

Describing Imogen making a portrait for *After Ninety,* her last assistant recalls that she would gently but firmly move "right into it, all the time charming the person. She'd introduce us both and then ask me to move the chair out of the way, or open the shades or pull the curtain. She'd always talk, make wisecracks, keep the attention of the sitter on her, making the person at ease and amused by her. Sometimes it would be all over in twenty minutes." Over the years many have agreed that, as Christina Berding wrote in 1951 in *Modern Photography,* "When you've been photographed by Imogen Cunningham, you haven't just had a sitting, you've had an experience."

Imogen's comments on the men and women portrayed in *After Ninety* reflect the attitude that informed all her later work which was, as Hilton Kramer of the *New York Times* put it, "the straight-forward address to the subject that places the interests of life before those of Art." Of the man she called Little John, for example, she said: "This man was a printer. Was. He's ninety-four and a farmer and he raises apricots. Oh, he's so amiable and you know what I said to him, 'You know, I'm coming down to your farm when the apricots are in season.' He said, 'Fine, we could use another hand.' "

No matter what the situation of the person, Imogen admired those "who were spunky," who did whatever they could to be active. Of Mrs. Fairfield-Osborn, who weaves: "This lady is in her late eighties, and she's doing a beautiful piece of work. That's why I photographed her." She had her impish sense of humor at work when she photographed Dr. Joel Hildebrand. "He's a chemist, and I asked him to put something on the blackboard for the photograph. He was delighted with the print and sent me his article on the viscosity of liquids. It's wonderful, but what do I care about the viscosity of liquids? . . . This was done in his laboratory. . . . Now the woman who went with me . . . she's a Ph.D. in a science and she and he talked all the time and I didn't talk to him much. She said, 'Watch out to avoid that one tooth that he has out.' And I took it, because I thought a man who's that old and only lost one tooth, who should worry about it? I don't think he'd resent that, because he has the greatest interest in the world."

She admired a pianist she met named Martha Eidler, who was over ninety and was refusing treatment for cancer after an operation. They talked about their agreement on the right to die: "I might as well die when I'm supposed to." There was the ninety-four-year-old manager of a large property who amazed her by posing on the horse he still rides; a famous surgeon of ninety-five who had just come up by bus from Mexico to visit his sister and forgot his appointment with Imogen the first time because he was up and out at six o'clock in the morning to visit friends; a high-school teacher of more than fifty years' service who was nearly one hundred—Jessie Luca, age ninety-nine, a lineal descendant of John Alden, who said that "she was a graduate of Mills College when they said prayers."

Maybe because she had spent part of her childhood on a farm, Imogen seemed especially affectionate in recalling the several sessions photographing farmers. When she gave prints to a farmer named Morisset (as she did to almost all the people photographed), she was given "cress and some lettuce. Then I guess he decided that wasn't enough, and he came out with a tray of raspberries. And, I mean, it was a treat. It meant as much from him as what I had put into it."

Recalling Imogen during that afternoon at their home, Arthur and Lillie Mayer concluded: "Well, Imogen's just an amazing woman, that's all. I suppose the work was what put her together, kept her together. It was one lifelong thrust. By the time she had reached that age, she and her work

Imogen Coming Down the Steps from Her Home in San Francisco
Photograph by Tom Eckstrom

were one." Without knowing it, they were echoing a prophetic statement by Imogen herself in her 1913 article: "Though a woman gains immensely in breadth and culture through a useful profession, she also gives something—something vital and energetic. Her face may betray the lack of leisure, may possibly show some of the strain of her work; but for my part, I cannot see that a woman of conspicuous leisure grows old more gracefully than does her energetic and creatively active sister. This is, however, a minor detail in the consideration of a profession—for any work which one loves brings with it a peace and satisfaction for which no amount of repose and elegant leisure can compensate."

Imogen did give something vital and was a source of energy for others, an example of a self-disciplined, hard-working, independent, forthright woman, who never wasted time dwelling on the past or passively waiting for the future. In her, students found a real-life artist who happened to use a camera, whose presence was a reminder that a long lifetime of serious effort in art can be rewarding in and of itself. Her life and her art are intertwined in a pattern of growth as natural as that of the plants she loved to photograph. If the process of growth can be thought of as a process of constant refocusing of the self, then Imogen accomplished this growth through the camera.

All old people are unusual by virtue of their long lives, but not many are original. The few who are seem to hide a secret which the rest of us, seeking answers to the big questions of life, try to discover. Imogen noted this more than once: "They come to me for the big word. I don't have it, but they think I do. . . . Why is it people think anyone else has the secret? There is no such thing as a secret—you just have to work and find your own way. Everybody can do it. If I can do it, everybody can." Despite the protesting, people came—students, teachers, photographers young and old, artists, filmmakers, friends of all kinds. Never a typically doting grandmother, Imogen found a solution for the potential loneliness of old age in her relationships with young people. She encouraged them—or discouraged them, sometimes harshly, if they displayed a drop of pomposity in their manner. One young man called and asked to become her assistant in the darkroom. "How long have you been doing photography?" asked Imogen. "Two months," he replied. Pause. Finally she answered, "Well, call me back in ten years."

Imogen, the photographer, took her work seriously; work provided her with community, self-confidence, and ever-expanding horizons, mentally and socially. Anthropologists say that the real achievement of the aged since the beginning of human community is to end their lives passing on the tradition of the culture to others while remaining independent enough to be useful to the group. Imogen realized this goal in a typically original fashion. Two years before her death, concerned with the future of her work, she established The Imogen Cunningham Trust to preserve her negatives and exhibit and publish her prints. In conjunction with this plan, she had a Chinese chop designed to be used in place of her signature after her death. The mark consists of three Chinese characters representing the name Imogen phonetically and translates into "Ideas without end."

Those aged who achieve and maintain an active and creative role rule with their wisdom (or, as in the case of Imogen, with wisdom and wit). While she disliked the label of queen, she held court nonetheless, alternately loving and hating her "notoriety," as she called it. Anita Mozley, Curator of Photography at the Stanford University Museum of Art, recalls the visit she and her husband made to Imogen in the spring of 1976: "We were there to look at some photographs. The phone was ringing every few minutes. Each ring meant somebody making a date with Imogen. Finally, getting on toward dinner time, three very attractive young men came to call and take her out to dinner. Off she went. That was the life she lived. That was her society. In fact, she really wasn't old to any of us who knew her.''

An artist like Imogen is one who does not waste time, motion, material, or words in whatever she creates. She finds the straightest line between two points. For such simplicity, there is no formula. In looking at old people, we are asked to see ourselves, for ourselves, from our own lives. There is nothing to copy in Imogen's life or work: no style, no tricks; no monuments to build. She was a person who was a tangle of contradictions, who resolved the opposites through her lifelong quest through the lens. She kept it simple. Asked about being a woman, she would reply, ''I am a photographer, not a woman.'' On the other hand she accepted with amusement the newspaper columnist Herb Caen's declaration that she was the new sex symbol of San Francisco. One might say that she balanced the tension of contradictions with an ironic wit, that ever ready weapon she knew so well how to use. Even in her last days she reserved the right to change her mind, to wield her indomitable wit once more. Her son Padraic tells of her reply to the preacher who visited her in the hospital a few days before she died. ''The fellow wanted her to fill out a form asking what religion she was. She raised herself up in her bed and she said, 'Haven't chosen one yet.' ''

There is energy in the expression of wholeness that we keep in our mind's eye of a person who, by being true to herself, not only made works of art but through the enduring vision became one. This image of energy has an emblem: full-flowing black cape; a crown: ornate cap; a jewel: silver peace symbol on a ribbon around her neck; a banner: her camera; and an expression: clear, wide inquiring eyes beneath a fringe of white hair. Her presence among us proved that life could be lived fully, savored even into late old age. She wore many hats, real and symbolic, including among them: cottage queen, comic-opera witch, hippy grandmother, curious child, researcher, gossip, intellectual, horticulturalist, gardener, cook, worker, comedienne, and, last but first, artist. While she was unpretentious as a person, Imogen was of a sophisticated intelligence, carrying a high standard of behavior, honesty, and integrity in work and life. Hers was a rare breed of a tough strain, a humanist with a sense of humor, one whose interests were as varied as her friends, and always growing. A photographer by trade and actress by nature, Imogen Cunningham could play all these roles; after all, she had spent ninety-three years acting them out, developing the parts to her person, creating at last this ageless, frisky, elfin creature, a crone in a black wool cloak, our heroine of the camera, bright-eyed, quick-witted, and working—even after ninety.

Margaretta Mitchell

After Ninety

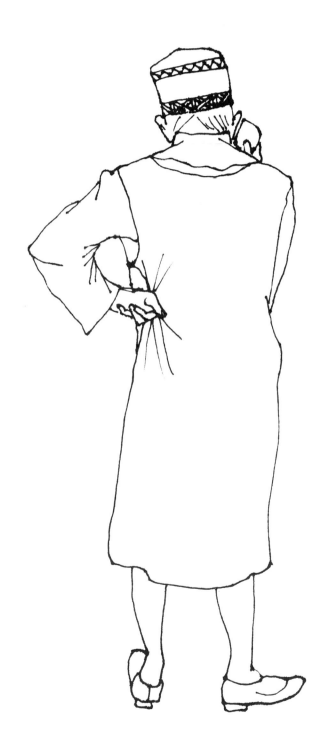

Imogen Telephoning
Drawing by Ruth Asawa

This is the entrance to John Roeder's shrine in
Richmond, California.

John Roeder worked in an oil refinery,
but was really an artist.

Here is John with one of his sculptures.

This man is an anarchist, and they call him Little John.
He's four and a half feet tall, not even as tall as I am.

Niallo was my neighbor but said he was sick of California.
He was moving to his in-laws in Texas. "To hell with
California," he said.

She was knitting a red sweater for her granddaughter because red is good luck to the Chinese. I stayed for a Chinese lunch, but it was too elaborate.

Dr. Eloesser was over ninety, and he came to my house to be photographed. I told him he should have no trouble climbing my steps since I managed it with my groceries every day.

*These are two sisters, ninety and ninety-four. I had to
pick out the clothes for one of them for the sitting. So I picked
the most ornate things she had.*

She was a high school teacher for more than fifty years,
and the banner behind her was done by her niece
to show her achievements.

That's Mr. Penington and his daughter, Ruth.
He was a hundred this year, and I was invited to his birthday
party on Fidalgo Island, but I couldn't make it.

He was a former labor leader and a communist.

This man had a dried fruit company. He's ninety-nine and very alive.

She is a poet and a painter, one of the founders of the ACLU and of the Presidio Hill Open Air School.

This woman taught art at Mills College.

He's a chemist, and I asked him to put something on the
blackboard for the photograph. He was delighted with the
print and sent me his article on the viscosity of liquids.
It's wonderful, but what do I care about the viscosity of liquids?

This couple was taken in the thirties in a hotel downtown.

The wife is a poet, and that's a book she just published.

He was the hardest man to photograph that I ever took,
next to Stieglitz.

I call this, "Age and Its Symbols."

*We used to explore the Sacramento Delta together
with our cameras.*

These were taken in one of the old Delta towns.

She said, "When we were young we were all puritans,
and all we talked about was whether it was right or it was
wrong. And then I married a man from Sardinia."

I took this at the Bay Area Rapid Transit station entrance
in Berkeley.

This lady is in her late eighties, and she's doing a beautiful piece of work. That's why I photographed her.

She was a famous pianist, and she's ninety-some.
She had just undergone an operation for cancer, and she
refused further treatment. She said, "I might as well die
when I'm supposed to," and I said, "You're right."

When I delivered the prints he gave me cress and some lettuce.
Then I guess he decided that wasn't enough, and he
came out with a tray of raspberries.

He's proudest of his potatoes, and he gave me this big one.

This man had a children's television marionette show
for thirteen years.

I met Tom Roberts, the puppet man, at an art festival.
He gave me a mimeographed book of his poetry,
and I sent him a print.

I was telling Dr. Cookinham my medical history
during the sitting.

This man was in the city engineer's department.

Of the group of prints of my ex-husband from this session,
the one he liked the least was with the cow's skull,
so I decided to include it.

I think Roi was moderately pleased with this portrait.

He writes technical books on photography,
but I never read a thing he wrote.

She lived down my street, and I saw her sitting in the
window and asked her how she spent her days. She said,
"I just try to get through them." She was nearly a hundred.

He was one of the earliest industrial designers, and feisty.
The last time I saw him all the fight had gone out of him.
I couldn't get him to argue about anything.

I photographed him as a job, you know, every two years.
He'd have a different color suit and a different shirt and
necktie every time you'd see him. He's the head of a
design school.

I took this the day after I was on a TV show in Hollywood. We hadn't seen each other in fifty years.

This is her husband, the sculptor, taken the same day.

She is a distinguished radiobiologist who asked me to
photograph her. I wasn't taking on commissions any more,
but I did it because she didn't care if she looked old,
and she didn't hate her face.

She's made her living all her life by collecting
California seeds and selling them.

This man is a retired cheesemaker from Switzerland.
He's so strong! He grabbed me and whirled me around the
room. He's a folkdancer, and he did a thing on the floor,
grabbing his feet and rolling and rolling.

This doctor was a public health director, and he sent me a
three-page résumé to convince me to take his picture.

He told me, "I never gave in to a strong impulse.
I believe in a golden mean."

*I took this famous European photographer at his house
in Germany.*

This rope maker worked at a lumber camp during the Depression.

I photographed this at an outdoor market in Finland.

This woman was in a home for the aged in Copenhagen.

A nap in the women's restroom of the public library.

Halfway through his nineties he still rides a horse
and manages an estate.

This lady descended from early settlers, and she's active
with the Mendocino County Historical Society.

Old Norton lives by himself in his shack.

Old Norton going out to do his washing.

This was at a bus stop in the fifties.

He was a workman in the Mother Lode country.

I took this in a compartment on a train in Germany.

This was in the Gold Rush country.

The three ages of woman, on Fillmore Street.

These were taken in a Berkeley "convalescent home."

*She said to me, "When you come here nobody knows
where you are."*

He didn't want me to take his picture, but I did.

This was the result.

These are the father and mother of Ruth Asawa, the sculptor.

This lady likes Indian jewelry.

This couple is Arthur and Lillie Mayer.
He's still teaching the history of American films at three
universities every year.

She was a great botanist, but she kept her office specimens
in mayonnaise and jam jars, and in tin cans.

This is Mrs. Bauder, the goat lady.

This is a guy I picked up in the post office.
He comes from Korea.

I couldn't understand how such a creative filmmaker
could be right wing.

This woman had been in the carnival all her life, but I found her in a hospital. It looks like lace, doesn't it?

She was a physician in a women's college and very religious.

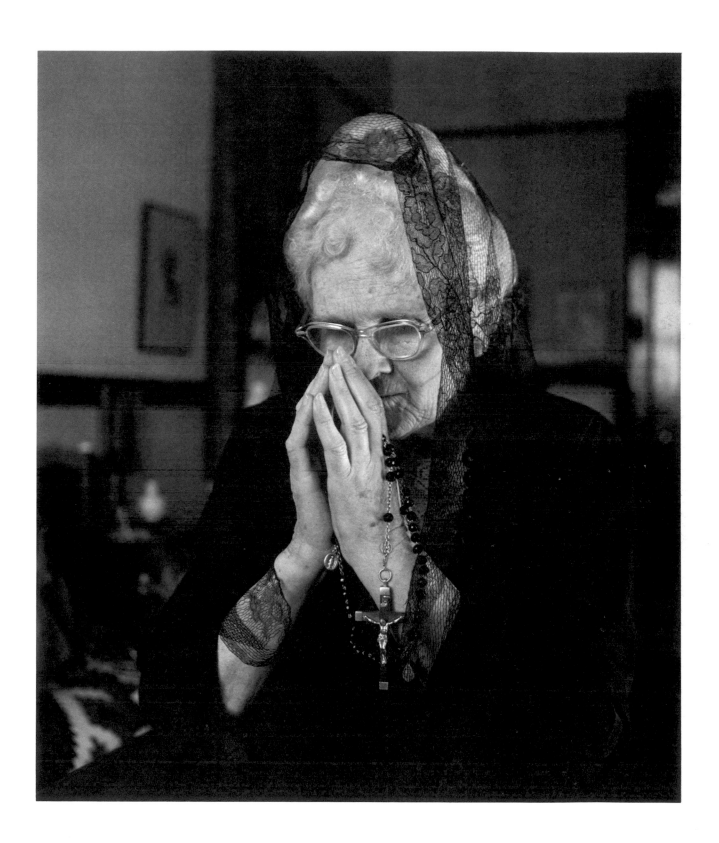

I took all of these nuns in a convent on the Peninsula.

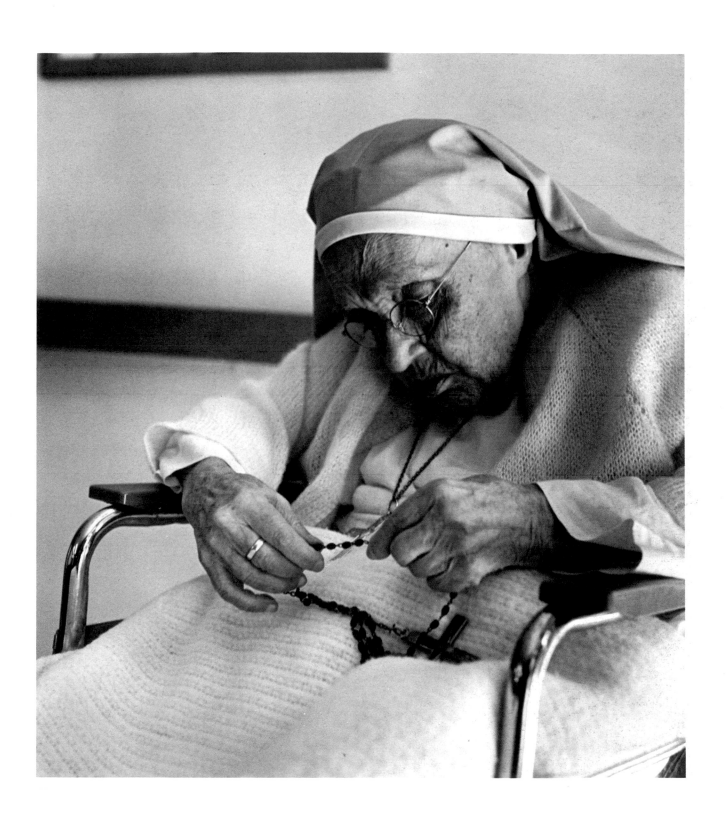

My father and mother.

My father after ninety.

Selected Bibliography

BOOKS AND ARTICLES BY IMOGEN CUNNINGHAM

"Photography as a Profession for Women." *The Arrow of Pi Beta Phi*, vol. 29, no. 2. Seattle: University of Washington, January 1913.

Imogen Cunningham: Photographs. Introduction by Margery Mann. Seattle: University of Washington Press, 1970.

Imogen! Imogen Cunningham Photographs 1910-1973. Introduction by Margery Mann. Seattle: University of Washington Press, 1974.

BOOKS AND ARTICLES ABOUT IMOGEN CUNNINGHAM

Anspacher, Carolyn. "Imogen Cunningham: A Portrait of the Photographer at 92." *San Francisco Chronicle*, 31 March 1975.

Baccari, Alessandro. "Imogen at 91." *California Professional Photographer*, January 1975, pp. 16–17.

————. "Imogen Cunningham." *Album* (London), June 1970.

————. "Imogen Cunningham Tribute." *ASMP*NC Newsletter*. San Francisco, July–August 1976.

————. "100 Print Show at the Witkin Gallery Celebrates Imogen Cunningham's 90th Birthday, 11 April–13 May 1973." Press release.

————. "Photographs by Imogen Cunningham." *Creative Camera* (London), July 1971.

Berding, Christina. "Imogen Cunningham and the Straight Approach." *Modern Photography*, May 1951, p. 36.

Conrad, Barnaby, III, and James Danziger. *Interviews with Master Photographers*. New York: Paddington Press–Grosset & Dunlap, 1977.

Daniel, Edna Tartaul. "Imogen Cunningham, Portraits, Ideas and Design." Interview for the Regional Cultural History Project, University of California, Berkeley, 1961.

Diamonstein, Barbara. *Open Secrets, 94 Women in Touch with Our Time*. New York: Viking Press, 1972.

Halderman, E. Isabelle. "Successful Seattle Business Women." *Seattle Post-Intelligencer*, 1913.

Hershey, Ann. "Remembering Imogen." *California Living Magazine*. In *San Francisco Sunday Examiner and Chronicle*, 26 September 1976.

Holz, Kay. "A Visit with Imogen." *California Living Magazine*. In *San Francisco Sunday Examiner and Chronicle*, 21 November 1971.

Kramer, Hilton. "Remembering Cunningham and White." *New York Times*, 1 August 1976.

Leeson, George. "An Exclusive Interview with Imogen Cunningham." *Second Spring*, August–September 1975.

Margold, Jane. "Imogen Cunningham at 91: Still Developing." *Ms. Magazine*, February 1975.

Maschmedt, Flora Huntley. "Imogen Cunningham—An Appreciation." *Wilson's Photographic Magazine*, vol. 51, no. 3, March 1914.

Rich, Judith. "In Focus with Imogen Cunningham." *Westways*, August 1976.

Torvik, Solveig. "Portrait of an Artist: Imogen Cunningham at 91." *Seattle Post-Intelligencer*, 13 June 1974.

Wiseman, Diane. "Imogen Cunningham 1883–1976." *Popular Photography*, October 1976.

Plates

2	My Father at Ninety	1936
27	John Roeder's Shrine	1961
28	John Roeder	1961
29	John Roeder and Sculpture	1961
30	John Cook	1976
31	Niallo	1973
32	Young Lym Wong	1975
33	Dr. Leo Eloesser	1975
34	The Brand Sisters	1975
35	Edyth Fredericks	1974
36	Ruth Penington and Her Father	1974
37	Carl Sullivan	1975
38	Yee at Marshall	1975
39	Helen Salz	1975
40	Florence Minard	1975
41	Joel Hildebrand	1975
42	Hotel Couple	1930s
43	The Laurence Arnsteins	1975
44	Clarence Burr	1975
45	Age and Its Symbols	1958
46	Griswold Morley through the Window	1963
47	Griswold Morley	1963
48	Jessie Luca	1975
49	Emmy Lou Packard and Her Mother, Mrs. Walter E. Packard	1975
50	Marjorie Fairfield-Osborn	1975
51	Martha Ideler	1975
52	Bryan G. Morisset	1975
53	Raimey at Marshall	1975
54	Ralph Chesse	1975
55	Tom Roberts	1975
56	Dr. Cookinham	1976
57	Eugene V. Block	1976
58	Roi Partridge and Cow's Skull	1975
59	Roi Partridge	1975
60	Bill Hawken	1975
61	Frances Chidester	1975

62	Jo Sinel	1964
63	Rudolph Schaeffer	1976
64	Rose Krasnow	1976
65	Peter Krasnow	1976
66	Maria Kolisch	1973
67	Lester Rowntree	1972
68	Fritz Steinmann	1975
69	Fritz Steinmann Somersault	1975
70	Dr. J. C. Geiger	1976
71	Augustus Locke	1975
72	August Sander	1960
73	The Rope Maker	1930s
74	Finnish Market Woman	1961
75	Danish Woman Sewing Braid	1961
76	Napping in the Library Restroom	1955
77	Walter D. Bunnell	1975
78	Nannie Escola	1971
79	Old Norton in Bed	1968
80	Old Norton Going to the Laundry	1968
81	Buy Rainbo Bread	1950s
82	Mother Lode Country Workman	1963
83	Woman on a German Train	1960
84	Gold Rush Country Workman	1963
85	Three Ages of Woman	1972
86	"Convalescent" Man	1975
87	"Convalescent" Woman	1975
88	Bill Adams Resisting the Camera	1951
89	Bill Adams	1951
90	Umakichi Asawa	1966
91	Haru Asawa	1966
92	Ruth Elkus	1965
93	Arthur and Lillie Mayer	1976
94	Alice Eastwood	1953
95	Grace Bauder	1968
96	Chan Doh Kim	1976
97	Karl Struss	1976
98	Irene "Bobbie" Libarry	1976
99	Dr. Eleanor Bancroft	1951
100-105	Nuns at Sacred Heart/Oakwood	1976
106	Isaac Burns Cunningham and Susan Elizabeth Cunningham	1934
107	My Father after Ninety	1937

Design and Production: Adrian Wilson, San Francisco

Production Assistance: Adriane Bosworth, Maria Poythress Epes, Myra Levy
Sean O'Donnell, Joyce Wilson

Photographic Prints: Rondal Partridge

Research: Danee McFarr

Technical Assistance: The Walter J. Mann Co.

Composition: Mackenzie-Harris Corp., San Francisco, in Centaur and Arrighi Types

Production Management: William James

Printing: University of Washington Printing Plant, Seattle

Paper: Karma Text

Binding: Lincoln & Allen Co., Portland, Oregon